(VICE) VISCERA

WILLOW
LOVEDAY
LITTLE

CACTUS PRESS
MONTREAL

(Vice) Viscera / Willow Loveday Little.
Little, Willow Loveday, author.
Poems.
ISBN 978-1-990474-09-5

Published by Cactus Press, Montreal, Quebec, Canada, 2022
www.cactuspresspoetry.com

Cover Design by David Drummond
Photo of Author by Christian Moreau
Interior Page Design by Devon Gallant
Edited by Devon Gallant & James Dunnigan

For Finn

It comes in waves

CONTENTS

III. Rubrication [Proof]

i. AN ANATOMICAL DRAWING OF VISCERA

1. Body: Old English *bodig*, of unknown origin.

2. Secret: late Middle English: from Old French, from Latin *secretus -a -um* (adjective) 'separate, set apart', from the verb *secernere*, from *se-* 'apart' + *cernere* 'sift'.

3. If you cleave soul and skin, is the result separation or affirmation?

4. Xenia: the sacred relationship between guest and host. The host must be hospitable to the guest and provide them with food, drink, and a bath, if desired. It is not polite to ask questions until the guest has shed their skin. The guest must not flay the host.

5. If you interpreted host in relation to parasites, you're speaking the wrong language. Let me translate:

6. The body only relinquishes its secrets at gunpoint. A gun is a chamber. A bullet-less gun is a corpse.

7. The body is sacred because it is round as a story. Conditions outside defy narrative and, thus, are inhospitable to Xenia.

8. The body doesn't lie.

9. Utterance is an act of vulnerability; language, the vein chosen to reach a heart. The orbicular oris is composed of four quadrant muscles, but the mouth is still more a circle than that, especially when screaming.

10. It is possible to scream silently.

11. How could you leave me alone in this unknown land? This glade, upended?

12. Manifestos are for little girls. Women are for evisceration. After, there are fewer barriers to Xenia—you can practically hold her hand through the curtain of entrails.

13. Denotation is viscera itself. Connotation is scalpel in skin. Connotation is everything going in circles. Poems are angular. Poetry is—

14. Sometimes, things grow inside.

I.
COLLATION
[SPINE]

ON PREFACES

Xenia, the truth is within
the book, burgeoning on the lip
of a word, but my language is my body
and my flesh, a morbid intrusion.
Understand. It was love at first sight
when he removed my blindfold's tongue.
Clamped into a reactive role,
I was culled until I couldn't
commit seppuku, couldn't spill
my insides into witnessing.

Cuffing lexicon, it ceases to bridge.
A period up close reveals itself a ball-gag.
This isn't a love story. This is how
restrictions breed creativity. This is
leather-bound spine
straining to touch
once upon a time to nose's worn epilogue.
A narrative arc splays dogeared pages,
corpse incorporates.

Everything he said was erotic. Left nothing
beyond the absinthe, candles, crucifix
and smeared tempera.
In the marginalia (which no one will ever see)
a foxglove extends its mottled question
into a hand. There,
a jungle beast's pelt
shed amid dehydrated wings of bracken.
Flowers wilt, and my appendix bursts—

You removed iambic pentameter, semicolon,
flesh-red ampersand—
Did you not read my dedication?
Did you not read?
Did you—

Language fails;
my responsive part one
where anger was tied between the teeth.
That shiny meat hook and all that he took,
and I who gave willingly.
The body gives up
what it cannot hold—

THE DIAGRAMMATIC AND ARTISTIC REPRESENTATION OF CANNIBALISM AND PSYCHOPOMPS

I.

We're taking it in with a newfound perspective.
My carmine legs encircle your own, which are (respectively):
the blue of Yale,
the Olympics,
iron-cast independence.
And yet, that unseen place where our cells imbricate
is a colour all its own. An RGB fever dream.

II.

Let there be two terms, x and y,
a whip-poor-will in glade and a fresh kill.
The bird's down looks like that of an angel.
Why? I'm not talking about set theory.
I'm including the soul, interpreting its route
to the ekphrastic, not casting it in judgment.
These are my terms.

III.

You're showing me a round.
On an aged grassland bounded by acacia,
we abandon safari crew and campervan.
Play "spot the sun-seared cloud."
Overlap gesso sky and ground
like fat from the skirt high up the thigh.

IV.

Take two. We're kissing by a painting
you drew me to, of waterbucks on ecotone.
Mouth so wide, I could be consumed
and rendered into something else.

V.

Our union intersects over game:
tapered gazelle, rhino, grass-fed giraffe.
Grab the rifle, escort me from the wing.
Where to next?

VI.

While writing the guide
Venn becomes a circle jerk:
one of those men who cares about you
in his own fucked up way,
someone who curates and cures his own meat.
Ma'am, you're standing too close.
Now I want Jack the Ripper to make garters
of my guts from the top of a double-decker bus.
I want him to corsage my wrist with sinew.

VII.

There's a mandatory tourist shot
strewn across the trail:
trophy hunter in red zone
captured with a catch so rare
it's practically blue.

VIII.

Missed the signs:
the sun a clot of light hanging in the sky;
the way he whispered
my entrails were too abstract to be fine art.

IX.

I said he hurt me.
He said, *Be reasonable,*
That's just a question of schematics.

X.

Figured,
the guide left me for dead
in a gallery, far from any national park.

PHYSICAL EXAMINATION

How many stomachs with Rabelaisian smiles must I stare at impassively
before the teeth are put away? [Code for the door please. Social, no digits. If
only it were that easy.] I conduct myself like electricity, though I can
understand why you thought music. I'll be clearer in the future. Fingers are
the key and I mean so literally, which I say because tone is necessarily
articulated for the colour-blind and cultured alike. [There's a knife edge to
my shame ought to be followed by a doctor.] Cut your teeth testing coin.
Fold guts nicely before you pack with ice, tummy-tuck them back in,
smooth wrinkles with steam. [I took an oath. Destiny and dropsy, dirt devils
and motes collecting thick as milt on the baseboards. Angel juice fresh of
the morning. The cut and the share. Love, a price that pays for itself.] When
slumber encumbers me, the dialogue is stilted: my stichomythia hindering
attempts to stick it to the man. [Is it hot in here?] I dreamt I held Xenia in
my womb and she kicked real hard. In sleep we retain what's drained upon
waking like lymph or seed. I just want to be good. [Is that too much to ask?]
Batten shutters so no fly-ins or aways. Here's something that made the
cut—pigs eat people. Dorothy's fear was real; does in my own of fertilizer
for poetic fodder. [Best muck it up.]

I want to be good.

GRAFT

There are pigs
magnolia blossoms crush underfoot
Slick mud visible below ice like blood
walling in a fingernail's quick,
and crocuses, camouflaged
against frost, whose delicate petals praise the sky.
I close my eyes in
answer
ears picking up gut string curlicues
the tails of tones wrung out
a soft orchestra backing
Antigone, begging to bury,
stones closing overhead.
This spring
chilled like pinot gris
trickled
down our throats
in melting streams of ice nettled from granite
by the sun's omnipotent gaze.
Everyone wants some-
one who looks
at them like the sun does
the Earth.
My galoshes, too blunt
caught hip height on stunted fence
grey as a child's sleeve sucked grey for comfort;
I barked my shin on
ery frame's cuticle.
Winter flushed bruise   ,
Crazy,   my hot cheek,   taste of tannins
an acrid bloom on tongue, speak the words—

                     too pink

belying

                        Elsewhere, the lilac

   that language
                   in prayer

dishcloth
   not orchestra*ted*
                   funerary process
  Rebirth.
                  demands flowers, not coins
back me up

choking us with life   rite on

     strip my skin to see the staff within
   bird's eye view could be
   binary to male gaze

straight out of a Nicholas Sparks' novel
my psychopomp's   xenia
crocus   counterpart   ferryman's lipped lilac
a nasty habit
     a   gnarled, nasty girl   The splint-
repeat the question, please
                  went red.

slaughterhouse slaughterhouse slaughterhouse

                  Spring's final answer.

FOUR HUMOURESQUES

I. OPERATION 101

Red bile: "You're so vein."

Asked to describe the victim, her friends chose "short and lively." Mortician went in with the makeup while I watched, the red making me see—like stars—clots in my coffee. Squashed tomato of a head wound needed stitches and bad, post-curbstomp. Tiktokked our search for her perfect wig. Recorded myself saying she comes to mind as a belly laugh—a magician plucking roses from sleeve, vivacious, perfumed, salvageable. An under-CoverGirl who loved Dvořák, playing the piano, a daredevil for the latest trends. Dandelions and litmus tests. Taken too soon.

Apply long-wear foundation, brush back the brows and blush apples of cheeks. (Not the chemical peel we'd originally planned.) Setting spray to last an afterlife, and presto! Poco allegretto. Now she sings from her diaphragm, so straight and eager. A stranger in a choir of angels. This is how they go— young, beautiful, and in danger.

II. FLIGHT OF FANTASIA

Yellow bile: "Papa was a galling stone."

Boarding the plane, bored of this hot, dry summer like a stale heel of bread I cannot bring myself to eat. I'm going back home, to the motherland—fleeing far this pain in my side. Compose the trajectory of the voyage as I take off, draw peppercorn stars in the sky, replace the hostess' hat with a chef's and demand sous-vide in a java-scripted jive. Dress codes and a caffeine high. Ignoring the seatbelt sign, I mind-control the pilot so we improvise my wicked way into a nosedive, materializing mountains amid clouds of meringue. We crash *and* burn the meal. This aircraft's just an old baguette repurposed for croutons. Imagination, the sincerest form of fantasy. Pretend that made sense, and you'll get the point. Child's play in perfect harmony. They'll pay millions for the black box.

III. RHAPSODY IN FIREARM

Black bile: "That offal sound."

Action

I am lucid enough to see it coming—all that distress, discarded jade plants overgrown their terracotta pots, slumbered flotsam of a schefflera's mane. I awake to pee and wash the nightmare from my hair, but it has nowhere to go. The space between each of your breaths is a fermata, every spurned snore the "to whom it may concern," letterheading the sleep I can't help thinking means my lungs are the body of the message. When head warms pillow I freeze; the music gilding my canals is the circadian click of a Colt striking midnight like a thief.

Trigger

I can't handle myself too well nowadays. Memories are backbone, black quaver on quires. This oblong is the time she didn't answer the phone and I thought she might be dead. That F flat is my brother threatening to kill him, and I distraught and ready to martyr until I realized he didn't have the cur's address. Welcome to my firing mechanism, my well-worn weakness. I comb out my hair and get angry. Resilience isn't my forte. Release the checkered grip pattern like you played it too sharp. Pull back the firebird pin.

Barrel

I could watch women shuck oysters for hours. The pearls fell from their mouths like notes off a hammer dulcimer—freshwater pink, trident green. Their eye whites were nacreous, propelling the gaze through time to where I sat, getting off on each delightful gem popping up among the bivalve carnage. Gauge how badly I need to not be in control. Should be muzzled and slugged, the polymer traffic of storage space overgrown with and by the wild, until it becomes automatic.

Bullet

I dream blood and guts and movement. Damsel fly in D Minor, tithes paid
in pins and needles. D.C. al coda. Repeat. Play it backwards in smokeless
powder yawning that devil's tritone, demonic messages, cult interpretation
birthed by physics and the hesitancy of a hand that says "should" is a safety.
Percussion lock. Conceal myself like a pessary, through Canadian tuxedo,
wifebeater, Axe-scented candle skin. Sforzando. Heat seeking heat seeker.
My modus operandi, understandably, solipsist.

IV. LULLABY FOR LINE AND VEIL

Phlegm: "Cold November brain."

Rockabye player on the tabletop. When you play X, we promise to stop. Nursery mnemonics of stories before bed, truss and trust, poison and hex, lest indeed, we do forget. Rest your sweet, frosting-white head.

Remember hard lines you drew with branch of elm or portals to forgotten realms. Softer limits. Inexplicit; the wax and wane of dungeons and dementia. You've lost yourself to win the campaign. The DM's got some kinks to work out of the board: cleric, bard, warlock, a lot of hurt. Sensitive topics we'll gauge in gauze, then wrap in the binding of your cursed grimoire. Safe words for the senile and aide-memoires. And if that horse and cart—

[*The scene cuts deep and suddenly all of me is spilling out, and I can't keep me in.*] Life force in stats and gulping breaths. Roleplaying death, I always thought of the red of blood—each singular drop exiting my heroic body, not this reality of losing myself in increments. Redundant alignments. My party's got me outnumbered and I don't know why, when, or how.

Said I was hit with plaque. Said with twinkling eye, "how I wonder what you are." Said trying to attack with charisma, I failed and took critical damage. Said I rolled slumber on two dice. It's getting harder to stay in character. Asthma of thought when the bough breaks beneath this adult weight. No saving throes. Slurring last words then slip to surrender. [*Hurriedly, the DM fades to black...*]

ON EXTISPICY

Mostly we are mondegreens, by which I mean we diagnose
meaning from each other's words which may not be there.

Is my red your red? Where you see symbol, do I see stain?
The scintilla of tinder visible in eyes sparks forest fire in heartwood.
Post-Visine, pre-dating apps, or perhaps read-eye from phone's flash
or receipts to sender. The words we tip down each other's throats
are supple limbs, and yet also a reminder
of a previous love's voice reverberating old bones.

My god, how the soul grabs for what it knows it wants:
phrases that ossify, the what-ifs of love struck down
by *I know*'s larceny. Knuckled petal of the dog rose,
depilated cacti, barely beloved blossoms, reincarnations
a bouquetful. A lotus buds from each pore pinpricked
to a pointillist fantasy. You're so goddamn subcutaneous,
I feel the heat from brutal magma in the impenetrable deep
beneath dermis. What waits unsaid shrinks
in the shadow of commandment: recital, the silhouette of name.
Speak it, and I might be free. Tenderizer, you trace my name
with your finger from hairline to haruspex across a pilgrim path,
along suicide crags to parted lips to end at my omphalos.

Are you God carving my existential crisis
in slices of the finest laudamus te money can't buy?
Can you read fortune from my sacrifice? Fate from victimhood?
Gloria, in ex celsis deo. (Your ex, Chelsea? Oh. My anxiety.)
Normally, I hate being dissected, but with a scalpel of my own,
I've been invited to return the favour.

It sounds cruel—to cut open—

But we're really just looking for vital signs.

ON CONSUMPTION

I'm a not-flag,
a limpid shamble of squared affection.

Amid greying steak and steamed chard
my pale voice becomes safe enough to digest.

On the television, a prince with kaleidoscope eyes
debates a DJ in a romper crafted from reconstructed mirror.
Voyeur and exhibitionist.

The prince shuts his eyes, and says,
It's enough that bulls build nations, but cows fit a convenient narrative!

Yes, but just how *aetiological is a sheaf of wheat?*
The DJ scratches a record with one glossed nail, absentmindedly.

My lover chimes in:
cow hearts should be sold in supermarkets,
the guttural lows of bovine love lit by fluorescent light
amid arugula, Romanesco fractals,
fingers of cucumber, trolley glint.
And of course, true aetiology resides within the grain's germ.

Meanwhile, I spear bloodless
between the blades of life.
I wave white and truce-like,
and pray I don't cut off my thumb.

AMYGDALA HIJACK

[   ]
[   ]
[   ]
[   ]
[Adrenaline flooded the basement   ]
[and stole the keys.   ]
[   ]
[In a grand theft autonomic,   ]
[I robbed myself.   ]
[Sleep paralysis at the steering wheel.   ]
[These dysregulated pathways, these roadblocks.]
[Choices I cannot realize,   ]
[clutch that won't be brought to heel.   ]
[   ]
[   ]
[   ]
[   ]
[   ]

ON PHLEBOTOMY

Vesalius,
was it treachery to turn your body bodysnatcher,
boil the criminal bits, question your god?
I question mine all the time to remind me he exists.

Galen was intravenous. Your wound grew
feverish with dreams of Pergamum.
The breathing vein gasps open
like a disembowelled monkey,
miracle of shambles, IV in the fourth vein
of the brain-play cow,
oxen circulating a Pan-flute syringe,
spring-loaded lancet, fire cup like a holy grail.

Even the porcine pieces hold truth,
though they speak a language unknown
to the sanguine orator peddling auctoritas
like medlars at the podium.
Might as well be glossolalia hanging
from their lips in puckered leeches
to those of us well versed in viscera.

To dissect surgeon from physician
is to go through life with half a heart,
to trust performance over evidence of animal spirit,
to cause half-blind harm,
to survive vivisection.

The emptying vein is an internal conflict.

Vesalius, did you humour him?
Brother, lover, challenger.
Can you kill a god by asking the right questions?

(DE)SHELLED

Forget the warnings of whiskered women. Futile murmurs
of jade-weary crones propel girls-next-door to action.
Forge rebellion from unwound plaits, paint revolution across lips
who boast they can wrap around three-syllable words.

She's bending forward,

pistachio ice cream dripping down chin,
proudly sixteen and a half,
to the greenest grinch:
varsity jacket, hand-rolled cigarette, unmovably gelled.

                    Baby loves him 'cause he's cold.

Paw under the bleachers because it's what the movies say we do,
and what sixteen-year-old doesn't want to be a film star?

Grass stains wash out is an excuse.

                    Roll your skirt, lean closer.

The murk beneath river foam clears.
Your legs, a divinatory pool, are a wishing well of skin
for people to throw copper pennies at, into.

                         You wonder at paraplegics.
Distill invitations to be aerated by eyes,
signed by your own cursive hand, sweet and dry.

When he sees his intent pour into your skin, it stirs in both.

                    Make the most of spring.

Realise kisses mean tasting the mouths of others.

                              Do these dips into the unknown
                              draw you forth even though you
                              miss your sandy cove, little crab?

Forever dreams last long as stubbornness lets them.

                              Crack shells,
                              scuttle one way, the other.

Later, you'll remember how the first time hurt—
how the Berlin wall bled,
how those grey towers crumpled to the ground
as if God had hit them over the head with a wine bottle.

                              Mind the cracks, all of them.

ON ACCUSATIONS

My pricked thumb pools blood coagulates a grapevine leaks a pattern swirls
a mirage of footsteps weaving as the body rotates on its axis taut as rope
taught me how to sprout accessed by the hands of the weavers beseeching
communitas from the suede carved from my back and tanned into assembly
into resembling a something human resembling a face like an oil leak puddle
is iridescent trembling is pareidolia is a butterfly wing is DMT is ink or
blood is the same thing as ink and blood as skin or walls boxing in
prehistoric vertebrae like the fragrant ribs of fiddlehead or Vaseline on
chapped cheeks or moths illuminated as manuscript post-flame or gasoline
fumes iridescence of the smell of vellum before it becomes vellum how
violently inimitable is a fingerprint is the dwarf from the fairy tale who
imprinted my mind when I was five and full of fairies one might say
impressionable who spins a ring of his hair a circlet fine and gold as this
circle we thread through our hands like Macbeth's witches stirring their
cauldron in the cleansing in the clearing the way the smoke machine shows
in the ruby droplets in the jostling antibodies of the liminal leaves bound by
blood as the stitches leaf through me in blades of grass and whet wherein
the conspiracy of group think and machine elf hold my rawhide seams
together medical-grade pulp spilling out threatening mea culpa in the
pointing of a finger.

VENA CAVA EVICTION NOTICE

Five minutes is all it takes
and then I'll be further gone
than I am farther from you.

What's distance where disappearance
concerns matters of the heart?

Carved hawthorn ventricle
pumps punkish blood into alarm-system
à la mode. There's a key under the dog-wet mat,
with instructions for those who can't

tell a cache from a mailbox

or refuse the layout of lawn
with its ryegrass sprouting tinsel
you'd decorate a tree with,
like you last Christmas,
homesick for a place you'd never known,
unwrapping newsprint facades
from a doll house's plastic.

A good tenant knows a house from a home.
A good tenant knows the law ought to   protect the tenant.

You were conceiving double entendres
and I, endeavouring to   eureka life   into the fireplace's soot ear
when the shaking stooped us beneath the table.

Cranberry sauce prolapsing impasto.

Brussels sprouts roiling broiled petals in the pan

like thistles in a storm.

Our trembling passed, remember?

The turkey had fallen in split-broom tinder
which might have been rosemary, another year.
The heirloom carving fork
which had punctured my father's lung
when he once mistook robbers for roommates,
clasped in my sleeve like a kiss.

Our trembling past, do you remember?

Cardiac arrest is the only recourse
for a holiday spent Home Alone
when loved ones lock us in
until we're tense, passé,   incapable of living in the moment.

                                   Restoring a ruin
                                   is the quietest form
                                   of extinction.

Keep the valves oiled. Keep the blood flowing
in the right direction. As I could.
As I could.

A good tenant is intuitively aortal.

Your hand chafes the window's calluses.
                    The wind wants in.

ON &

They had to remove metres of gut:
punctuated colon. Puncture wound.
Mad dash to a reddened vent.

     Cannot absorb into bloodstream without ampersand.
     Cannot trust intuition without ampersand.
     Cannot flatworm hole to hole

without ampersand.
Without ampersand, Galen means nothing to Vesalius.

Without ampersand, no gibbet-thief gallows fear.
Without ampersand, pig suits homo sapiens in the flesh,
stunts modern medicine. No connective tissue,

without ampersand. No synaptic threshold. Trojan horse
loses the gate when ileum's no longer on the map.
To "bloodlet" becomes an attempt
to house a tenant in a vein.
Satanic clause never was   because

                no alleyway bicycle figure-eight

affirms with contrast, the light against the dark.
No childhood fight.
      No scraped knees, lessons learned
           without ampersand.
               There's no way to digest.
                    Murex-stained dog maw.

Predicate season. The cut-off before dawn.
Without ampersand, neither cleave. Never us.
No conjunction results unmetaphored. Unversed. Eclipsing

this cancer, ellipse sutures red ampersand.
Solidarity, only a syllable set.

Cannot be lonely if unknowing.

By itself, beetroot, kidney bean, watermelon pip.

THE BALDWIN AFFECT

We learned to smash snails, their millennia
shells evolved only to alter, now, on the asphalt.
I pick a grey muscle from the rubble,

pluck out its eye, and let my gullet
conjugate it. Emphasis is my natural selection
within the backlit terracotta of crucible

cave-in. Shellshock. "Offspring" has no
past participle when you hold it right;
flexed, it shines like a noun.

Our inheritance is instinct, on top of which—
I'm a fast learner, inflecting glut, so my beak
glisters with gastropod, looking like the real

missing link. On feather-lit porch, I bird bathe
in the gene pool's pink basin. Waggling
like a post-piscine diva,

my grammar's too poised
to seem a pretender, antagonized by
the empty agony of appearing less than

present continuous chickadee.
Watch closely. This is me.
I'm authentically passerine,

faking by making,
adapting with such speed
it's like there's been no lesson.

THE BUTTERFLY EFFECT

Can I recapture that moment, recapitulate how one letter changes
the meaning of a word—affect to effect, only seen but never heard,
smile to sneer? A butterfly spurns a flowerbed on the other side of
the world and I awake, sweat-slick with trigger warning.

Morphos fill my dreams. Shiny blue tailcoats, wishbones for antennae
blown afterbirth-damp, too damp to snap with a dream at my lips.
They thresh in a cold reserved for cover of dark. Hospitable chaos.

After, I came to expect moths. Shiny mandibles clicked in embarrassment,
sutured my sorrow away in ruby stitches, a linguistic miscarriage from
one "no" where a "no" should have sufficed. Inches of intimacy spoken
too close. At the cost of a wrong phoneme in a carefully calculated game,
I lost everything. The price of deciding to be a warzone is *being* a warzone.
The scars will turn you crepuscular, into a chrysalis sensitive to the
profound and widely divergent effects of love at first oversight.

All is aftercare in love and war; no survivors means no allies.

Wish I was mollusc not moth—
could puke up my stomach to free these stalling butterflies
so their gold fans flood the dusk. No wonder kids sift drowned iridescence
from rippling pools on summer mornings. Initial conditions mean a drain's
microcosm crystallizes maelstrom. It becomes a whirlpool demoted.

I'll stay a fluttering thing startled from afar, clammed shut on the knowledge
that oil puddles are attractive to the eyes. Lepidoptera, tornados, Texas.
My wings manoeuvre their delicate ailerons wavering on surface tension.

Dream stillbirth until I stop this palsy,
until moths no longer mistake the flame for a moon,
until an organ donor cocoons free from the fluid.

ON VERTICES

Speak an ocean free from sinusoidal waves,
swim curves that affirm the moon's wandering gaze,
drown in a crescent of wine-dark sea;

entry appeals to me.
The spoken word is a promise; thus, inherently
unfulfilled. Complete the circumference:

Rebirth the midnight glow
of a lantern fish tessellated within the shoal,
voyeur when taut drumskin eclipses the frontier
of some undone country. Fuck the vertical.
I hold degrees in the interior arts. Could stomach the linear,
but prefer my tribe; I roll with medieval queens
cloaked in furs that umbrella inner dragons.

Here the gun's steel chamber,
the red arpeggio of bullets hit by light.
You spit lofty theories from the flanks of a levelled plane
but I'm in its trenches. My lips are distant stars.
Zoom in. Up close, a corner is becoming a flat spot.
Welcome to where I skin the story, scrape
margins aside, read between the lines,
and see beneath the hide's bristled edges.
How pedestrian, when the "pointless" rounds a bend.
My friends would describe me as "heliocentric;"
nightfall is the sun playing fetus in my cells.

Baby, what's your sine? I tell fortunes
from the amputated language of empty refrigerators,
horoscopes from a vowel held in the mouth.
Female posturing is all about the right angle
and I core myself every night before bed.

Each sunrise, Bluebeard's confession falls
into my ears, pools amid his memento mori shoeboxes
while we discuss which of his choices I'll kill.
I plot his pulse, point until his hypotenuse breaks,
and so the story sings my song. I'm never wrong.

I've had all the Dick, from Godzilla to Godot.
My insides are the perfect cache for a safety deposit.
Find me in velvet hotel rooms where Joan Baezs
write about spliff-smudging Dylans
who lurk condom-mouthed by phone booths
droning into notebooks, dulcimer-sweet
from strips of papyrus swallowed to coat blushing throats.
Their guts pitched too erect to ever truly know.

Listen for a tangent. That vanishing point's lips—
tearing through the graph to speak.

ON AUTOPSIES

Xenia,
it hurts.

The hangman tightens his rope
against this morning,
funnels it into your name
fern-noble in a green that dimples noose.
Xenia. Taste the air—its resin, its cure.
Each breath is preserved by miasma
as I traipse a red carpet of my own making.
Religion exists only if it is performed,
and I strut accolades,
a printshop girl
with Academy Award armpits.

In truth, I'm proudest split open on a table.

The morgue goes beyond—gets authentic.
Its formaldehyde tongue is curious.

A master apparition,
surgeon with a priest's bedside manner
carves a Y-incision in my chest,
a spreading yew tree whose
blackened resin extends into genesis,
vitals opening to confess their shame,
the scalpel's glint a last rite:
bone saw and winking forceps
anomalies discovered like
some Harrison Ford in khaki shorts,
lassoing himself through dying filament,
a portal to the organized chaos of anatomy.

When you have been slain, the body remembers.
Blood rings oasis, marks the garrison's bridge,
pales the lush desert vegetation in mosquito's breath,
and extinguishes the firebirds who brand golden apples,
gasoline-plumed. Their beaks forensic.

Rigor-mortis is the body's last defence
against surrendering its secrets.
Xenia. They're coming. Listen close.
The most dangerous thing about me
is my need to be a martyr.

A clot of earth. My spilling. This limpid coma.
A bent-browed father gives me away,
a new mother fleshing trauma against my ego
hammers Passiflora into my palms.
Something old, something new.
A resurrected adage.
Powder me noose-bruise blue.

I blush safe words,
a bride shedding her skin
on the wedding night,
trembling kernels of aurora
from oblong mouths of evening red,

as if she didn't know.

ON PLOT TWISTS

A forgotten joke wandering the heath
roused by a pulse beneath velvet tomb rot
waits for someone to tell her, bares her teeth,
and smiles like humour's just an afterthought.

Unvoiced, the set-up, the symbol, the drifts.
Unvoiced, the cackle, the staging, the verve.
A labial slab of marble lid shifts,
and Calvary sings like an ulnar nerve.

Funny, the dust stilling her coffin birth,
the barrow breath that resurrects the wheat,
the wind's laugh burying chaff in the earth
where winnowed corpse-keepsake crumbles in heat.

When punchline rolls in its volta,
you've made a grave mistake.

ON SCAR TISSUE

"None of the others bid me do that," he said in surprise.

Seven shirts, snow-white, she shed,
our rock-ribbed pharmakos.
Exiled to the honeymoon's yawn,
straddling the saddle of fate's forked tongue.

The bridegroom writhes, neglects the bedside Bible
and strips ink like a palimpsest.

His body is a fable,
figment of muscle—
Orphic, ophidian.

His stare, cold-blooded myth.

Each banded skin disrupts firelight—
strikes iridescent scutes into the EmberGlow logs
as the molt scales him back through time,
foreplaying a familiar crime scene
across the floorboard.

She's getting under his skin.
Hell, healer. Victim. She knows the risks:
infection, constriction, ego death.

Self-surrender. The touch of denatured silk.
Back home, she owned a snakeskin clutch.

One shift, vessel, a last lace slip
and he comes undone—
the fabric of the human body hisses, seethes,
and unbinds in seven sheaths.

The epidermis goes commando,
inverts its sashimi cuticle and rouses internal rabble
to break free from incommunicado, break free
from the spell, break free
and unbridle raw cognate.

Behold:
a mass of stretch-marked marrow.
Ugly and tarred.

The skin truly is an organ
(and vice viscera).

Scathing clean brush
in holy water,
she peels back
her last layer
of maiden oath, scrubs
python from man
with patience and lye,
and burns them both.

ON INSIDES

Unhook the bland sky like my dress
which in collapsing reveals
firmaments of quahog shell;
taupe rings, wet blue-black at night until
sunrise roiling seismic—tectonic—heaves apart chthonic crust.
You are sybil, sifting through the silt of alluvial deposits,
mining colander for accumulated ore of katabasis.
Something to nix, to grip by the throat.
Then zip back up the seams
of diaphanous heaven's azure fabric,
to hide like an egg within.

ON BRIDGES

These teeth are headstones.
These pink gums, graves.
Could carve an angel
from all this enamel.

Exhume a filling to discover
a mountain of wildflowers within.

ii. PROGNOSIS

The body gives up what it cannot hold
onto.
Entrails that go on and on.
I could go on and on and on.

II.
FOLIATION
[LACUNA]

FLORA

Nature walks through woodland's tract.
Retrace steps. Retract into
a bramble of blackberry stains.
Cuckoo's spit foaming on the stem,
frothed germ of life steadies inside
this cuckoo spit my father says is amniotic
with its sacred bubble-wrap phase
a child's curiosity must not invade.

Four years old and I'm all wonder
at the grub's flicking from
sun-gilded leaf, a finger's snap personified
as the cutest bean—
onomatopoeic.

> I prefer
> baby talk
> over
> eloquence;

The secret is
the forest is well-spoken.
The secret is
words are secondary to language.

Bluebells, honest as gas-fire,
allow their decumbent sung sapphire
to bookend the meadows
where encyclopedic bacteria flower.
Nearby, a gut-gurgle
babbles home to Babel.

My vegetable laughter. Father's hand, womb-warm.

Stone bleeds of lymph guerrilla each sunlit artery.
  An organelle peeks its resistance. Balsam bladders pocket trunks,
   weep sap that I finger to souvenir forest grime,
    an amber residue soap won't wash off—
     a proliferation in green.

Mud cakes my frog-faced boots
  on a copse-hug we call the King's Descent
   where a broken boletus crown has begun to ferment.

    I look up and gasp, let go of the stranger's hand.

Groping grass, I deracinate genera and disturb soil's gerund.
I'm lost without. Through the otherland, rumbles.
Not a wood run, this biosphere, IBS-polluted (nothing grows here).
A season of pink bismuth cultures forest.

    Pepto cloys gut feeling. Regress, repress, repeat.

There's a woodworm-nozzled fence, a back-door biome paged in gloom.
Silence mosses the lopsided rope swing where hunger reads like loss.

   The forest, unflinching amidst formula feed.

Read my lips, ten years down the line—
the orphan flowering multitudes beneath scrolls of birch:

I am legion.
I am colony. I am colonoscopy. Yes,
     I reign.

Between the verdant spires of my soul, flay bark to find green within.

THE NIGHT IS YOUNG

Behold as champagne moon   wipes me
against its genes   like a disk drive.
Its glow-dust organic   orgasmic
     as hip grinds   gyrates
coffee grounds
          euthanize me
               into suddenness.

Constellations   a   quinine tang, one
too many   I leave the splashed black sky
wet with purple stains
          from drunkenly spilled stars.
Little girl dreams   debutante dares
slosh my g&t   and carefully consider
sloe berries, how they ferment into   something
so   see-through,   permeable as
virgin
       gin   liquid   glass.

Streetlamp beats nightlight
   in popularity contest   every time
once reason uploads   parchment-sturdy.

     Yet tradition grows sterile,

pours itself another   short circuit-
analog round
        white dwarfs in its eyes.

Recognize the biology of time:

midnight the perineum   demarcating days
          rather than the hand's movements.

Soon   she burns ebullience
        until   only hard data remains.

Keyed   a caffeine hangover
dreams   dares
                        blasé babe
          gazes at the moon—
just another lump   (blackthorn stump)
of pockmarked cheese

                          lightyears away.

WHAT FOLLOWS NEXT

Undulating lamppost. Resounding halo
corroded gold by internal ruse. The field work still fields calls.
The clouds become mother, hanging loose on laundry day
while we wait for pressed pants and best silks. Animal stem,
in sleep remembers past lives, yawns with mute endeavor—
catches cranial lurch, then swaddles you close to cushion
against crunch. Narcoleptics anonymous change into new blazers
for lunch. Scrape off their roadkill, huddle in napped fleece and graze.

I'm going home. The pavement's delirium tremens is suspect
as coin-counting at the cash. Addict shudder. Hand encloses pin,
enamel blackbird. It's an amulet from Grandma to clutch
in great times of need, an heirloom of her husband's PTSD
from back in the day, before refillable grenades. This brooch
clasped by his same cold hand. Nowadays, they get you with eco-bibles,
anemic poppies, foot-long sandwiches, music heavy on the concussion.

My engine snores. Something afoot: me.
Skidding through public gardens, banana-peel walking side then faint,
sleepiness beckoned in streetlamp where's pasted a newsprint protest sign.
Missed merino coat, pricked skin, blood cambered like fresh
currants across billowed glass. Wings of detergent, washboard dream.

I could have sworn
two birds trilled
You were only hallucinating
in the dead of night.
Then the fall,
post-lapsarian,
totem vision totalled
by an obliging metal pole.

RUIN, LEGACY

She's supposed to be resting. If the terracotta catches her eye, she'll travel
to a faraway land, decorticating lamp shade from evergreen and impressing
my mind's marble as I clear the table. She hasn't lost hers. Her fairy tale

is one of survival. The oppressor's cardinal sins, her directions. Frye, I
think? Northern. Blossoming syllables alchemize Cinderella at twelfth strike.
A maiden name trails—like pumpkin vines—chapters of tail between legs,

contusion bloom whenever his gaze dared slide muddily into the charming,
and beneath the floral canopy, she pulls free like a roll of birch, milky and
raw where it defied defining. I'm in awe at the agency of landscape.

Its emptiness. Its hostility. How she exchanged a set of letters for escape
across a wilderness, as necessary as those three saplings tended half a
lifetime, their pea twigs budding in a framed photo. I replace it gingerly.

She is a sighing tree syrup-tapped and marked, who stretches tired limbs in
the bath to soak its bark. The omission in this foundation myth is what I
learned. Post-apocalypse, metal crates drown in rust but you can

forego the limits of genre. Writing what you want is *but still strong*.
Her handwriting happily-ever-afters through our family in a root system,
wisteria wiring column like a broken jaw, bursts of hysterical pink

recognized for their boreal calm. Oh anima. Resin insignia drips to mark
territory with conifer, to needle the forest floor—the garrison's lexicon
drifts back to the bunker. Survival's a start. Identity's close.

Undisturbed, a flaming maple chars the sky with its victory signals.

FAWN RESPONSE

First run, second freeze.
    I don't know how to fight, never thought
        to be cross. Sometimes, trading your clothes
            for mid-winter camouflage is all that's left.

I drop my skin for a mottled pelt,
    metamorphosing into someone else—quadruped,
        innocent, my black eyes a plea, a
            fig leaf of a tail tucked between legs
                like Bambi at his mother's funeral.

In the woods they shoot me down,
    carry my corpse to the field
        where in early dawn they slaughter me,
            gut me, butcher me into portions
                then packed in Ziplock bags.

        The sun rises on a bloodstain of grass
        painting snow where a crocus
            has pushed askew an empty beer can
                as it struggles to grow.

A year later, my slayer chews marram in a pub.
    He has fresh kill in his eyes.
    I will courage to my lungs.

I hold my skin
    clutched tight to my breast
        where suffocates a single pressed flower
        snug in my bodice.

You used the animal. Meat to decorate your freezer,
bones to stew for broth, stories to glory in.

You used all of me
so I had to change
into someone else
and so I became
someone else, something
and still you used me up
and I recall
when I was small,
seeing a bird on the feeder
clawed down by cat,
how it seized to be,
transformed instead
into a non-thing
like what you did
when you used all of me—

Not a swath of cartilage thrown out,
nor thread of sinew discarded.
All my marrow strained, served, savoured.

His smile a knife, sharpens his words. Waste not, want not. (Such a clean
cut.) Gambrel of spine straightens, and he massages my shoulder to wagyu,
hums, "Be a good sport. Pink suits you."

My ligaments dissolve; cloven feet glued to the edge.

He says

                         the hunt is a figment of my mind.

                                   I buy him a drink.

EXQUISITE CORPSES

Dearest Heart,
We were ambling up to the lookout, which posed against everglade
like brachia in the city's black lung, when I remembered our body.
I stifled my breathing till it paled, grew weary, left
the sugar-barkled snowbank alone. There was something corvid to the sky.
Something pinioned. Outgrown.
Some thing divulges our destination will be other than fisheyed cityscape,
rust rail, buildings lit up like a motherboard.
I swallowed words whenever you paused and began to stray

toward that matchstick woodland where I won't.
Is there something you want from this winter night?
A curse lifted or boon restored, a logpile to commit
your pyromania to? Snitches get stitches
but I'm good with a thread. Glimmers reveal.
Shadows are invitations I rescind. Belly of whale
is where secrets ferment. Lay them in the snow

for the moon to mend. Puffs of condensation leaked in the chill,
tangled in trees, froze. A slimsy crow
knocked clouds off a branch.
It lowered its ragged beak to peck an eye from the ice.
The diamonds were gone. Her hair, a curl of mute
paparazzi gold. The Versace gown bought
last June was a snag sunk in the bog,
a bough submerged in that damp winter moment,
reduced to a feature of dusk's idiopathy.
I looked at you, and the thought crescendoed,
broke my visage and welcomed your shock—
Why had she come alone?

                    Though I knew,
                    I wondered and meant it.

ON HABEAS CORPUS

The unrecognized iris reminds of the fractured, the favourite, the fond.

How then, the now, the niche between your eyes?
The kind, the burial shroud, or the resonance fatigue?
How the drainage, the channels, and body of water,
when flesh acquires the status of imprisonment?

My mother, with her dark hair and moon skin.
My sibling fauns with flammulated crowns.

What then,
when bones no longer register trauma,
When eyes without cataract turn cloud?
To imagine death is to imagine a lost eye in your navel,
to try to see the same darkness with judgement's axis mundi
as experienced only in sleep.

The keyword is "try." The insane darkness.
The navel-gazing. The vicious circle
of nature or nurture and who hurt whom.

As experienced in sleep,
a telescoped attempt.

HALF-LIFE LOVE, HYPHEN

Cross purposes veined like the rib of a leaf
          cleave our green blade summer-long.

Gather grammar of tree rings, bleaching coral, filo folds of varve.
          Hyphens connect word to note.
In our ruin, we cling, stone-enamoured lichen.

I'm aware of in between the in-between,
          ring-around-the-rosy a chain gang,
our carbon-compound adjectives caught
          like the linear progression I sought this July,
run-through like a Hamlet.

Out my window, the atomic violence of the horizontal line
          pens the strand ink-black. A prairie harpoon. Across the
sunset: cosmic rays react, ionizing hawthorn to a forgotten henge.
          An open gate, a rust-lipped hinge, my tawny cardigan
thistled by type. Hand in hand. Past the trellis, a rose ribbons your shin
          like chiffon.

Historically, I've dated all isotopes,
          from the archaeology of fermented ocean to charcoal,
from dissolving femur lugged from the peat of a marsh,
          to aging sources of sedimentary rock,
from an antler's worried velvet,
          to the hypochondria of words halloumied in wound.

Integrity's not the forte of a radionuclide,
          so I let go.
Nowhere to wander on a Roman road,
          and so I slipped unity's umbilical tie,
a half-Windsor tress, Pratt, four-in-hand.
          A slack grip freed his rose-gold noose.

When I die, it'll be one-worded,
                      unpunctuated,
pure and nucleic—
                  defined only by the grooves in my bones.

The echo of modal is a coronary bypass,
                  divided in two, a split-tongue middle.
                  The likelihood of regret forks before receding.
Coulda, shoulda.

                  Beneath the nuclear reactor's light,
that night on the beach
                  I gave you half of me, took half of you.
Heart swift as an arrow, abstracting the required time
                  for a quantity to reduce to half of its initial value.

Half-life, hyphen. I will have loved him.
                  Severed and sutured and seen and sawn.

IT FIGURES

The bottle of bitters licks its own rim
and dawn recasts my duvet's dark as ceiling.
Vaulted origami of cathedral is a paper fortune-teller at rest.

> Sleeping on the right side of my body of work,
> where Tuesday flits in to flirt
> with the garbage truck's trowel hum,
> is like sic'ing amnesia on Memory Foam.

Yesterday, I was countertop, a horizon
between the lonely crucifix of kitchen chassis
and beer can's flat. The wall stretched PBR shadow to pier
and I saw a body of water, a punnet—

> The candle killed itself. I spat out seed, along with reason.

A body of rock exists for the chisel. Its preoccupation is with outlines
not entrails, those ropes with which the living hang themselves.

Eventually, jilted grout pinkens to a crumbling pedestal.
Today, I have nothing concrete to offer.

> *Sometimes I dream of you—squeezing juice*
> *from a silver urn, slung-kidney wineskin across*
> *your midriff. Hibiscus blue, steeped Ferrari red.*
> *Distance makes the heart grow fonder,*
> *your knuckles brush thimbleberry; I grow stronger.*

The hourglass resolves. When I guess what you're thinking—
I'm right more often than with friends
whose silhouettes I'm entitled to know.

LICHTENBERG FIGURE

I.

I am a maid fell in love with a storm.
If he hears my yearning, heeds my words,
I will rename myself in silver.
A blunt boon of atmosphere.

II.

Carageen blisters to coral reef,
feathers in threads across my skin.
The budding rumble short circuits my hourglass.
At last. Lightning flowers. A blossoming refrain.

Lavender's blue, rosemary's green.

III.

[dilly, dilly]
[dilly dally]
[dalliance to alliance]

'Twas crown shyness. Branching sceptres beneath the canopy coronating
a four-poster bed. Though timid in courtship,

        tear-stricken and meek, the scansion of thunder
        rolled closer, and you split a rock down its middle,

a sintered record of your intent,
like a rose laid at my feet.

        Wet ozone your favourite cologne.
        Rain, the sweat audible in dark.

        I wear you as my sleeve tattooed into a lanced-
through heart, evidence
of electricity begotten
by the camphor crack,
crystal stream, the ambling light ambered

        and spat back out, into my mouth.
        When you are king, I shall be queen.

[A talisman to protect from his ilk:
plexiglass, electrum, beaming sun,
tripoli-softened plectrum.
Rub me with fur, rub me in silk.]

IV.

And I shall make him a cambric shirt,
so striking it will be. No finer needlework
                    there ever was than these words I clothe him in,
                    bespoken into being.

With the robes come the rules of ascension
which applied directly to the skin,
                    resolve into earth.
                    With the robes come comprehension:

The cloud-to-ground route bridges ego,
reigns in St. Elmo's fire for the soon-to-be-drowned,
                    directs the path of least resistance
                    as the toaster marries the tub.

                    You are the guide, I am the rod.
                    You are the law, I the word.
                    Your lichen, my ministration.
                    You, sword; I, blood.

Parsley, sage, rosemary
and even after all this time,
my vertebrae tremored
by frissons coursing spine
in bonsai trauma,
I'll admit I find you striking.

V.

Definitions: two.
[The sudden discharge of accumulated sexual excitement]
[The sudden discharge of two electrically charged regions]
Synonym: sky and earth.
Folksong the weather man never predicts—

VI.

Into the bitter tunnel of my lover's ear:

a whispered discharge.

VII.

Statistically speaking, nine out of ten survive
being struck by lightning. Mark(ed by) my words.

VIII.

I know thy might. I know thy heat—
I hear it in the shepherd's tone
when I climb the moors to pull wild heather.
I'll scale the cliff tethered to heath
until I hear your throne.

Baa, baa, black sheep. Have you any will?
The swell of ache is a Sisyphean steep.
Remember me to one who lives there.

[Do Androids charge their sheep while they dream?]

[See commands: weather]

IX.

The bleating flock can sense it coming. The cliffs' flat
        is stark against my height and the lace of my nightgown
                shivers in anticipation of potential organ damage,
                      internal burns, the risk of holding a god
                            in all their gold,
                                    permanent injury from allowing a live wire
                                      to jump your bones.

Choose.

                            I conduct your siren song,
                        your painting of alien ferns across my flesh,
                  REM sleep musings,
              mirror-image thoughts of the self-similar.
            Scars make the best mnemonics.

X.

Entry.

[Entity. Subtitle. Impact.]
[Absolute power corrupts absolutely.]
Interrupted skin: ruptured capillary.

With rings on her fingers and joules on her toes,
she shall have power wherever she goes.

XI.

He is my charge.
Cataract, courage, the scathing hurt
of the image overexposed.
Fractals for the amnesiac whom
I'll mend with herb, with volts
of my love and bolts of sky
to wash away with blue the livid,
whorls of lavender to sop sap from wound
and third-filigree burns with salve I'll soothe.
With rosemary for sorrow,
I'll rinse the kelp of his minnow-bright hair
and remove the static to recall
the pine-pin storm's gambol over my skin
until he is well again,
for he once was a true love of mine.

XII.

[the death message appears: <player> was struck by lightning]

PLACEHOLDER, I CALL THEE BY THY NAME

I.

Axon in dendrite forest.

Look-see
over a shoulder disintegrating to gypsophila petals—
                              before this space,
her suspense of snow settling to salt pillar.
Aarne-Thompson C330 grade boulder, perhaps?
                              (Neither time nor place.)

II.

I can't stop shaking. Years tracing
the lorem ipsum of my sheets,
                    that fossil touch of hair on pillow
                    compressed then into cheek.
Names feel like weight. My tongue
gives way to the hedgerow of rhyme.
One epithet for all nuance of kings.

III.

I'll go back for that later.
Leave the cramp as it is,
visualization, routine—
the smell of slang, lipid duvet, insulating smile
                              of a friend's teak words.
                              The nerve, the nerve.

IV.

And here, its synapse.
I'm dowsing for you everywhere I go.
Until the drawbridge's myelin

                snaps, frayed
by the faulty wiring of a euchred sun
collapsing in its ochre setting.
The rooster crows at morn.
Dying's not the fear—
I won't be a cliffside,

                crumbling to chalk, cocaine, plot foil.
                Not twitching bulb's palindrome
                making Bell blush.

Nothing but loose change
easy and thoughtless in the hand.
I'm standing by a gravestone,
a baize-framed placeholder
for what I can't hold.

V.

Golden bird sings in the king's palace garden.

Beyond lidded eyes
                    I catch the dancing water
                                      in the greenest wood.

If a body rejects you while you're dreaming
and no one is around to see it,
did you truly *belong?*

VI.

Subject-skewer,
they grew you from gypsum
a stone plant   a statue who gave   in flower
one last baby's breath.

VII.

Father, I'm glitching,
bent fingers the cow with the crumpled horn.
It's a shame I'll find it—goose girl, golden egg,
the clithral heath of the idiom's sheath.
I'm afraid I saved you a seat.

VIII.

Who healed Cock Robin?
Who healed Cock Robin?
I, said the barrow
with my soil marrow.
There were bones, a name.

IX.

For now I'll leave it
felled across the footpath:

[Illness]   Placeholder
[John Smith]   Placeholder
[Boon]   Placeholder
[Description]   Placeholder

X.

I lie in a field
huffing buttercups,
clad in nothing but memory
and my tightest Spanx.
A noon placement test
for how well this summer engine fits.
Temporary.

XI.

Glial cell birthed me; mother raised me.
Placeholder held me peripheral till I died.
Little Jane Doe buried me beyond the decimal point.
What a pretty bird am I.

XII.

[

]

Fare thee well.

MRI CEREBRUM SUITE

I. Northern Hemisphere

Repetitions of landform flickered
like a flip book animated in a child's grip.
Through the window against the cold morality
of which I pressed my cheek,
the tablature of transit measured
because of its fixed points,
in arctic logic, far from the equator of an hour.

Pterodactyl of a raptor coming to rest
on a pylon like a geometric Aztec made me miss the city,

its pigeons gutsy mid-dumpster dive,
the maiden spliff smoked on fire escapes
unspooling sapling shoots of smoke,
the strife of pavement slip when rain freezes.

Here, the melt. They gave me five of seven, you know.
Brain damage. The malarkey of arithmetic.
I might add, the car's a clavicle slamming toward
a later point in time. Hours extend in steps
of highway, falcon-dappled sunlight,
tamped yellow hyphens punctuating concrete stretch,
the texts I didn't read—with intent—before I left.

       No, the function.
       They gave me five of seven. We don't go back.
       Be it lifestyle or strands of DNA,
       this is the route, the constant.
       The car's clavicle ossifies in fossil fuel,
       revving synapses from bones of long-dead dinosaurs,

propels me forward. Glance
in the rear-view mirror minus two.
The car's injury. Five anger. You and I
have something to work out
against morning's paranoia. Collateral data.
There's a traffic light ahead.
Hit the gas until we're right.

II. Corpus Callosum

Cross the bridge dividing
sunrise from specular lake

Stem from steam
                              hemispheres
                 east and west

I fold the horizon
(down its middle)
a Rorschach blot

At night
sagittal lands
are unsaddled

                              seen in ink

twin swallowtail lungs

III. Southern Hemisphere

What I left behind is approaching
from a different milieu,
an encroaching peripheral,
electrical storms and overpopulation.

I approach from horizon:
caddis fly, cause and connect, the surface tension
of a lobotomized tear, nematodes toeing
the meridian, belaureled paraphrase, the wired
epilepsy of collective.

They were two and they were all mine.
I held them to my melancholy,
kissed breast seeing meandros in the whole of my milk.
Missing duct the in between, cobalt catharsis,
lapis pole mild in its sympathy waters.

Few translates to algorithm of amusia.
Damaged goods. Pop science says there's no such thing as bad…
Gutenberg. Read waterlogged, sorrow literacy
the result of emotional intelligence.

Read the cochlear unspiralling of vegetables
as I prepare supper for two, two. Carrot skin garbled
by garburator. Sinkhole in kitchen
sinks. The doctor frowned,
a cyclone of orange trope onscreen.
Points. Point please.
(That's not my arm—it's my daughter's.)

Read damage like a Coriolis force,
clockwise Coriolanus countered,
damaged when a school friend
scoffed at art's survival value
in favour of scientific accolade, and you acclimatized,
damaged, forgave and abandoned me in my hour of need.
Dropped caramel stuck

in warm holistic. Unsung heroes of Asclepius.
Socratic cockerel shouldering
the burden of dawn. The arm was here first;
I don't know why it is cold.

Sonnets performing open heart surgery.
Pass me the anapests. Clear.
I want a CAT scan of that synecdoche. Gestalt. Gestalt.

Would you have me false to my nature?
My better half, my bettered.

IV. Frontal Lobe

Biker king ploughs sulcus, dropkicks asphalt,

      the Sylvian grove
      a fissure of verb applied.

Hell's angel, homunculus
measuring gains in motor cycles

      thrilled by the bite of bitumen
      from an eternity of switchbacks.

I once watched a man light a cigarette
from the friction of the road
against his speeding car,

that strike of phosphorus,
match dying in reverse,
door thrust open to god—

as the driver beside him gauged risk like a surface.

V. Parietal Lobe

In dungarees and buzzcut
Prisoner Fourteen is sensitive

        to the touch.

Stimuli athlete,
clearance for Brodmann Area 3
requires his presence at orientation.

        A tray of acid, laudanum, barbiturates,
        burrs in his side and laudable effort,

the room bigger on the inside
than to the doctor it seems.

Alexia, read to me.

The syllabus between his fingers is an experience of proprioception. Its muslin is curriculum, a semester's expectations. Like a dream, he thumbs the cellulose, uniformly cohesive, and feels himself in two places.

VI. Temporal Lobe

Recall the impression of love: the input
of negative fifteen and moon
forming night, that your hair was wet
and he noticed because it was winter,
and said his spirit animal was a timber wolf.
How he recited a poem from memory,
which you came across a year later, splintered
by the coincidence of finding it again,
suddenly, like you'd found your heart, and later,
cried yourself to sleep.
Gnostic you gripping a friend's arm, chin bucking,
"it *does* happen,"
your brain's reward circuit affirming his fawn reckoning.
The remedial scopolamine of myth. Remember
kaleidoscopes— that you're only
remembering the memory of the memory, and each
episode echoes along the mind's mirror,
for your hippocampus sings spinal chord continuous.

Past stumbling home two months after the declarative
case that he'd forgotten you was encoded, drunk
past your bedtime, and the talk
with your grandmother on the temple steps.
Corinthian column present and so tensile.
Remember you can feel this way, at least,
even as reflections cut you like glass:
Seahorse of a locket quoting his neck. Wax-encrusted
absinthe bottle. Limbic pike of acanthus. An agnosia of
labyrinths happening too soon for love to make sense.

*He lit candles. Beneath a tree whose leaves spread a penumbra across
the bedroom, his bullish stance was burnished gold by the flame. I lay
back. A guest in his home, the importance of politeness dawned on me.*

"Do you water that plant?" I asked.

He said, "I'm a good god."

VII. Occipital Lobe

You had a vision of land furrowed from discarded foolscap,
scribbled on, junked, tossed, and left to roll like tumbleweed,
> each dry ruderal seed a wrinkle in the draft of dead grass.
> This beach where goose and barnacle are barbed by taxonomy,
where black geese chuckle as they spawn from their stalked filter-feeders,
and the pebbled striae are smooth underfoot, is a place out of your reach.
> A saccade of definition. Think fast for a prophetic hybrid,
> feathered crustacean with sea-bird genes.
> Bathing in ventral streams,
your focus is on the what, not the where. Again you fail to locate it
on the General Reference Map. See their genuflecting bodies,
with black-and-white barred wings,
> limp the coastal path up from tidewrack, nesting-twig wreath,
> their webbed feet enmeshed in fishing net?
Neither flesh, nor born of flesh. Medial cross-section.
Walk the nave which divides pews like a caesarean,
> the miracle birth of a death lionized. Open sea Frankensteined.
> This irony of no dorsal fins. The falsest dichotomy,
> Dionysian on both sides.

> *Dura mater, keep my nerves at bay. On that plain*
> *where the wine is sucked straight from wizening grape,*
> *I look to you for sustained eye contact. Vine and retina,*
> *compass and sign. Mother, the lingual brine spouts*
> *purple from its cortical fount; The blind lead the blind.*

VIII. Amygdala

I rend my sheets waiting for a bell to toll.
Too dog-dark for floral. Too old to be a brainchild.
A whimper foregrounds the incomplete, the dying—hold on.
I'm killing time…

…staked on my bed by myself. Self pale as a white dove as a curl of
parchment or perhaps pages curled within ringed binder.
There's these on my finger, but I'm missing the one I crave.
Sound of bells or landline down the hall.

Please can I speak to King Arthur
when he was small, anonymous as a fitted sheet,
a body-bag boy-mercenary,
Roman named so long before stone dared tempt sword
or the motion of pulling?

I could oil pull all evening,
swill coconut to dislodge deposits that wouldn't,
pull men I don't want. All saints' Eve and no Adam.
Lady of the lack. No wand summons.
No blade materializes over lake surface…

…Your pagan ruins. I'm sharp as a tongue.
Wit can be sword-sharp when chiselled

from the experience of being struck dumb-blonde.
I'm a Persephone the wind eviscerates
through the gusting grate's all-teeth smile,
white dress dyeing to bleed pomegranate seeds
which drip down thighs into ankled poplar's reach.
Seven year hitch in my long-term plans, it would seem.
This knowledge is my validation, this breach
my chainmail maidenhood. Marilyn, my woe.

It makes no difference which bits we concede as long as we connect.
I nurture. You are ruthless. Quenchant to tang—pain that sings.
Our Stygian waters are the truthful grey of things locked away,
of yin and yang mingling silver-screen scrambled eggs,
Gordon Ramsay adding crème fraiche,
Ramsay Bolton saving the shell for the hounds,
and here, me imagined birdlike: My eggs aching in my belly
of the whale, best round table around…

…All I want is to be your girl,
fixing you a drink or psychologically. Every girl dreams
of taming a mentor—civilizing him out of the bestiary's pages,
to flash synaptic, to know myself through your rebirth, to be yanked
like Excalibur from granite so I gleam and, held aloft in your Trojan grip,
reverb female, to welcome you to post-coitus or Camelot,

to soften you as I've forged your need,
to be knighted as a structure hauling the framework of our home
while in user manual's engine the cupid moves,
his pudgy pink limbs sweat-stained
as he runs the hamster wheel,
wings brown, slick with motor grease.

While waiting for you, I come to Bethlehem
to track the footsteps of Jesus,
but instead found Rome,
after finding only the prints of paws fresh in sand.
I bridge canine and salivate at the closest vibration,
remembering dogs sacrifice independent thought
for a master's touch. Call it love.
Call it neutered neural networks.
Alzheimer's of the wolf.
Collect call me
Cerberus, Cavall, Capitoline she-mother.
Call me "neuroplasticity,"
as long as you do.

I found myself walking in circles, wondering…
Jesus, Arthur, Riothamus, then Remus, Romulus—
Always the "us" trailing off track. Classical conditioning
I'll wash from my hair as the violins shriek.

You never text me back.
Heat creeps as though programmed
into my cheeks during the next scene
where I unlock my phone
and realize you've left me on seen.

Until my feet pestle hardest stone to glass,
my calluses will be palliative,
become talons like I've pissed off a god,
my bed spirals to underworld of a robin's nest,
my eggs sing themselves lullabies unhatched,
fluttering pillows abound like a slow montage,
stagnant in this yoni where nothing happens
into a coffin birth. Experiential bird dog.
I call my other parts chaste, free them
of the studied narrative like pulling skins,
and mine ever flaky as shedding prepubescent down
in favour of feathers.
Light as a—

You are absent, your absence ashes in my mind's urn.
You, enigma. Me in feeling like my mouth.
I'm the one who's been tamed,
A welt of a wildflower, panting like
Pavlov's goddamn dog.

IX. Golgi Apparatus

Cisterns of ambrosia packaged and sealed
while workers forego the bathroom break.

Got the factory line down to a fine art.
Vesicles filling valuables like we spill our hearts.

The cargo arrives at the cell tower sodden, its cardboard musted, tape peeling from ducts. The question blistering everyone's lips: burnout or union, which will we manifest?

X. Pineal Gland

I watch you unfurl like an archipelago / world ocean / host

XI. Mirror Neuron

Your story is dark matter:
speculation over macaques
like a diamond saw cuts

then reflects a blossoming sky,
North scar to light the way
a dislocated joint

lit against journey begun.
I understand your particles
as my own constellation.

The consternation of silvering,
the petals twisted to home cloth
speckled like amanita, I forgive.

Do you feel my silica
inside your breaking?

Bundle neural bindle
I carry you to you

XII. Wernicke's Area

Aphasia mists tungsten mountains

Their evergreen chain

a phrase disrupted

Cloud-peaked tongue—

I was unheard/ uneviscerated.

STILL LIFE

Ink lake across an Austen sky heaved,
threatened to tip to cliché. The dawn coughed itself into colour
like a bullfrog searching the vug of its throat for chorus,
and I wondered how "the world is magic enough"
could be seen as anything

                          other than agreement.

Muddling the mint of early conversation,
I sought you in a field one morning
where the spears of nettle—
plucked flags regaining their heraldry—
brushed my bare thighs.

                          Heretic. Invasion.

Unpruned, the stung prose became a wild body, and
the thrust of causation shook its exhaling green.

Freedom to is freedom from. I can't help
but begin where we've always begun.

MUSINGS ON IMPOSTER SYNDROME

I.

If it doesn't hurt to remove, you're better off without it.

II.

I echolocate through the crowd,
the impressions of velvet dress, puffed cigarette,

jeans like a postcard after it rains.

Stimulus that allows me to triangulate.

III.

I'm mute at the silhouette of conversations. Silence becomes
a process of suffering for beauty.

Chiroptera rags. Growth of gecko stub. Something to removing.

Concision itself is a lexicon of culling: wolfhound to pup,
talon to nail, susurrus to static to peace.

In the interim of pickled sunlight:

samphire in the marsh. Black walnut allelopathy.
Green inhibitors among the tolerant, a snake shedding
the garden like a skin. Removing creates new.

IV.

Forgive me—art, anther, lover, sin.
Do you see me over here, doing my thing?
My lapidary is less lap dance than signet ring.

An animal print bustier, haloed in halogen
in the storefront window I pass heading home
recalls the performative ethics of leopard eel,
fox print stamped into foot path,

                            nettle expressing its milk in cast iron pan.

V.

When it's real, you have fewer words and photo evidence:

dappling beneath the coral, red belly, full flash.

I always take off   my genetic makeup before bed.

The audience loves a morning-after opening:
mascara waking,
shed plumage of a bird that lost the match,
nuclear fallout on lower lid.

Sixteen lashes for my trouble.

Sixteen candles.

Sleeping is a performance of trust.

When I say "sorry," it's a clarifying clause.
Sorry is another way of saying I love you; I am grateful

for your attention.

VI.

Silence is the clearest form of concision. Most silent
when I dream of daisies, their necks craned like beading
microphones. Loudest when contagious.

The best lies hold a kernel of truth.
My art is clipped too close by too tired eyes.

VII.

I weep at dawn, the sunrise creeping
into my cheeks a false positive.

Pink in taupe room seems a blush.
An infection waiting to happen.

ON ANTEDILUVIANS

The lower the number, the less virus in the blood. Numbers range from over 1,000,000 copies/ml to undetectable.

Still I hold fast my integrity

Undetectable means fewer copies of the virus in your blood than the test can measure. In Canada, an undetectable viral load is usually defined as less than 40 or 50 copies/ml.

Skin for skin yea, all that a woman hath will she give for her life

Undetectable does not mean that you have been cured of HIV. The virus is still in your body.

Touch her bone and her flesh, and she will curse thee to thy face

People who are engaged in care, take anti-retrovirals, and have an ongoing undetectable viral load are substantially less likely to transmit HIV to others.

Dost thou still retain thine integrity?

Studies show that people with an undetectable viral load do not pass HIV to their sexual partners.

Thou speakest as one of the foolish women speaketh

FOOTNOTES ON DETAILS THAT FELL THROUGH A CRACK IN THE ARK'S DECK

1. God and the Satan make their bet. When they seal it with a blood pact, only one palm bleeds.

2. It was a time of great wickedness. A time caught in a vice grip.

3. The Satan carries a burnt match with him. It scars his hand when he tries to light it.

4. Research shows blood runs thicker than water.

5. Trans: Not stigmata; Styx.

6. The water has a curious sheen to it—X posits: has blue ever looked so red?

7. Parting your legs, counsels God, is akin to parting the Red Sea.

8. Taking the Satan's pulse, Job discovers a riverbed along the arm, tucked into a vein.

9. What a magic trick! Doesn't even smell like iron.

10. When God isn't looking, Job asks, "Why do bad things happen to good people?" The Satan replies, "The same reason bad things happen to bad people."

11. Our suffering bone-deep. Our grief too dog-dark to be floral.

12. The body does not lie.

13. Why the Satan lights the match is the wrong question. We all light matches, now and again. The Satan drags the match across a wall. It scars his hand, but he doesn't care. The Satan is a translation, not a man. He smiles. The match smiles back. The burnt match has the same name as Job's daughter.

14. Xenia, the best endings are always beginnings.

iii. HYPOCHONDRIA

Poetry does not connote. Poetry is detonation;
have a stroke—an explosion of metaphor,
each symptom a fixed point against
the belly of proverbial wisdom.

I could go on and on
caught in this vice grip,
this connective tissue
of where I am and where I've been.

First confinement, second, third…
Three, the humblest pattern for the host—

The first established sickness.

III.
RUBRICATION
[PROOF]

XENIA'S OATH

I swear by regalia and apotropaia and organon and gorgoneia and all the viscera in between, making them bear witness, that I will fulfill this oath and covenant:

To withhold from dissecting she who has taught me this art and to live my life in partnership with her truth and if she is in need of hospitality to clothe her in my own skin, and to regard her gifts as equal to my sisters in lineage—that is, our blood line—and to teach them this art if they desire to learn without covenant or sacrifice; to pour libations and wash their feet with rose water, to provide oral instruction as befits those whose lives are measured by the cycles of the moon, and all the other learning to my daughter and to the daughters of she who has instructed me and to pupils who see truth and have signed the covenant and have taken the cutting oath according to my law, but not those who wish to stitch curiosity cabinets of their abdominal cavities.

I will not seek revenge. If I can do no good, I will not cause harm. I will welcome all travelers into my home, ensuring they enjoy heaped platters of meat, the fullest glass of wine, the most oxygenated plasma transfusion, and the best seat to dine at the operating table.

I will not cause harm. I will provide information when asked. I will euthanize, but never through petrification. I will give a woman an abortive remedy should I have pennyroyal, angelica, or rue growing in my garden at the time, if she should request it. She is my guest, after all. In purity, I will guard my integrity. I make no claims of holiness.

I will use the knife as I please, even on sufferers from stone, for the gorgon's work runs deep and the pathway to vulnerability is one paved with the flint we chip from our flesh, and all guests really want is to be seen and known for who they are.

As a guest myself, I will visit homes for the benefit of the sick—meaning myself—for treating you is treating me. I cannot therefore vow to remain free from all intentional injustice, as my cause is selfish and for my parts, I have absolutely no interest in engaging in sexual relations with the host, whom I'd prefer to see inverted like a flower for her benefit.

What I may see or hear throughout the treatment or as I cross the threshold of the host's home, I will keep to myself, knowing such things are shameful to share outside the bounds of the caul and thus must be buried deep within the folds of my stomach to keep her safe. I am guardian, caretaker, psychopomp. Never thief.

If I fulfill this oath and do not violate it, may it be granted to me to enjoy life through art, being honoured with fame that is mine alone; if I transgress it and swear falsely, may I be sundered permanently and locked in a dark box, where no one will ever know.

ECONOMIC CYSTEM

Measure worth in menses, staggered cycles hydra-headed,
episodes which split and burn. It was a lump sum
of numbers and dates, pistoned for parlour games, payment,
making good on promises advertised on late-night television
that leaves your eyelids heavy and your abdomen in recession.

Happiness in resource management. Energy allotted
to hybrid warfare and hot water bottle compromises
that showcase their comfort en lieu of labour divisions—
troops sent to the wrong field to erect walls;
acetaminophen making the world axis spin and stop.
Adaptive expectations a theory of festering tension,
so it seeps into places it has no business seeping into.

At the bank, my money was in the wrong accounts.
Traded so wrong the city stopped, ran an exit route.
I blocked it all off, my shirt come loose, tortoiseshell buttons
skipping like cowries on the highway's onyx surface.
Hazard signs, fluorescent orange, and barter systems
with no body language.

It wasn't like I misplaced myself.
A war of distribution where each cyst is a bomb
and I'm a third party with no interest
in the evening news.

FOREIGN BODIES

post hospitium:

Waiting room magazines are an old trick:
busy the body to distract the mind.
My friend had her placenta powdered
then compacted into pellets her husband
grinds by hand while the baby cries braille.

My friend is blind to everything
but soft fontanelle, baby smell, and infant fists
she reads with her fingers.
Rolls joints of the brown stuff to taste herself
when she needs to see the future.

My belly tastes volatile—mercury more than miscarriage,
millimetres of liquid glass, iodine, pillow slug,
stable contact angles, the depression that
ghosts the inexperienced.

ante hospitium:

Painting my belly with tempera,
I cracked eggs and wondered if my art
would stick better with home-grown ingredients.
Too much pigment though—too much red—and Mars
wasn't my chosen subject, on top of which,
I certainly didn't want to be limited
by the irregularity of the moon.

Wish myself water soluble too. Impermanent.
I cauterize an ochre freckle, replicating
challenges, not DNA, and catch my brush
on the outskirts of the solar system
having dabbed with the same precision
I exercise when engaging in rough sex
or eating breakfast
in his clothes the morning after.
Spill yolk on his favourite dress shirt. Stains are
the second-best reminders.

This universe never expands beyond a big bang,
and I'm trapped; I wax and wane
perpetually.
Counselled I have no skill
for the subtle strokes on stars,
I let myself cool
and empty.

interim:

As I waited for the doctor, a crumpled horoscope
found its way to my hands, where it proclaimed
Gemini the most fertile sign of the zodiac.

Actually, Aries' ram horns curl
into ovaries and sound the same.
Aries. Ovaries. Eggs over-easy.

My wounds are pure astrology—
all prescription
and self-inflicted wisdom.
The glossed page that followed had an article,
"Eleven Latin Phrases to Make You Cum"
and I remembered how once,
we lay like two rungs of a double helix,
curved into each other, and I could see a nucleus
budding in the pupil of each eye.
Maybe the meniscus bow of my back
wasn't enough. Maybe it looked
like deceit
from the outside.

Now it's antihistamine make-up sex,
a nota bene (*mea culpa, mea* cum *culpa*)
tacked to my wall with desiccated bubble gum,
broken mobiles with crumpled moons,
post-party depression,
black hole clinics,
presents for glum baby girls,
artificially pink and planetary wombs.

Remembered, the early rituals
of sloughing a new lover's distance away,
one with whom I was celestial
as he roped Bailey's Beads across
a truth so naked we grew luminous
over talk of names, childhood,
the ethics of homeschooling.
Who once said,
"Hold me close—together,
we're a creation myth."

Barometers, glass stars, things shoved inside
with hope that they grow,
the black of expanding entropy—
These strangest things ER doctors find.

RESECTABLE

"The dinosaurs were expendable," I say and watch his eyes
narrow like a vein. Watch him calculate my margin of error.
I'm a sample he's processing, imbedded in paraffin
then put on ice like a Blue Point at an oyster bar.

Confidence is a clam's yawn at low tide. My words cool
with the charm of a surgeon at brunch. A proper lady
has good bedside manners, but he wants me on his laboratory table,
between vials and Bunsen burners where he can slice, stain,
and examine. Reminds of Mile End hipsters perfecting sourdough.
Buns in oven. Sticky fingers with a silver tongue.

Maybe what needs removing is less yeast than cancer.
If I'm going to have second-hand smoke,
it won't be a hand-me-down.
Memories can be: Mummy in the operating theatre,
yelling at the doctor, *"Just take it all out!"*

Excised the dinosaur joke from my repertoire.
Let's cut to the chase—does talking about extinction
make you want to cry or procreate? I always buy presliced bread.
You can examine its microcosm piece by piece.

REPRODUCED

Except that I'm one degree green of whichever coordinates
let me write liberation, I'm watching the clock.
My youth is ornamental. "Sort of" softens the blow
of a sentence, resists morning's clenched jaw.
I woke and rose like a water lily,
the geometry of my petals
unfolding fractals of pink snowflake
up through the H2O. I
rose like a rose is a rose is a rose,
a capitalist dream for the lower case
that never fulfills, only
we know we become our parents
and yet still we do—
dominant recessions, polymorphism in scare quotes,
a hormonal cesspool recognizable for its waters blued
from simile and chromosome. What would Monet say
on the subject of verisimilitude?
There is no conclusion today,

only curiosity and the will to change.
Asexual reproduction, cells copying cells
copying cells copying cells
still parented by two,
the semelparous grains of sand
silting the pond's baseline like semolina. Leaf
margin's semaphore.
There is no "I" in Gertrude Stein's
rose. Just a stigma. There's an art to middling, or so I'm told.

I'm not trying to be anything.
Anything other than what I am,
derivation of seed. An individuated clone.

Nymphs throw their gametes to radial gods
whose sex cells market padwise
on pollen in the wind,
genre's cage, where genera plays tricks
on the mind, shows root's only path,
the rungs scratched into time
with indestructible tights, a laddering tine
in the genetic helix.

Annual, perennial, millennial,
rhizomes and rhyme—
Perfect timing you could say, but only after.

HAEMATOPOIESIS

Knit scarf a bur itchy at my neck, I shuffled penguinlike
along the murmur of ice engulfing dirt patina, wary of slipping
as I neared the pond's polished callus which gleamed its opaque

off-white in a taunt at my skateless feet. Slip of a thing. Slip up.
I could be a salamander unveiled in mud, purpled miniature
parading her kingdom, could be red-shoed dancer compelled to whirl

on ruined soles, a girlish soubrette who giggles despite the blades
carving their name in her feet. Dare I say, the greatest monarchs
live in their minds—butterflied vision, symmetrical as day and night.

Wound pinked the bank as dawn drew and quartered the dark, quietly,
spilling corpuscles likes motes in the sun. I traced in cursive
"Here Be Dragons," with one long, ankle-shaking glide and felt
some song pounding my temples, some gut-strung instinct to escape
tethering me to a moment that could suddenly speak.

Mad libs for mad kings, hangman for queens. Knowledge privy
to the storytellers and bulk-order resellers: sword is greater than pen
until nib wins the award for least-expected knife. Sky a tarry smear
hemorrhaging ink. My glib grin a fiery thing.

HARVEST SONG

O Harvest Moon,

Tarnish nail to dirt crescent with your scythe,
spade bloodied taproots loose from soil grown plump

on shell, bone meal, the telltale clung-ruby
of plasma gorging land. Moonlit, silver tubers

bite the hand that feeds them,
like children ploughed prematurely

from mother's breast. Readied for transplant.
You like the live ones best.

DARK RED GLASS

Mosquito alights on desert arm,
lowers needlepoint to sip at oasis.
Ichneumon drills for promise land too,
dowsing bark for grub tremble.

Heart pumps blood into sap,
sap into tears, tears which dry
like a rosary, resin beads in protest,
which protect the broken vein.

Afterward, the telltale amber
reminds me to prey before I eat.
Not so different, the predator's ruby guts
from the victim stilling its pulse
to evade the prophet.

BODY COUNT

[

    1. A rag of branch in the pond, currant-coloured, swept off

    2. Storm cloud stored in gull's grey wing

    3. Thunder, which brays

    4. Leopards bounding across the water, their speckles flashing in
        dappled light

    5. Wind blown, amoeba shoal

    6. Placard flotsam yellowed blue by depth

    7. Usnea tassels like tinsel for nests

]

On the form:

    1. The body under the bed

    2. The body inside the bed

    3. The body inside the body

    4. The bawdy inside the body

    5. The berry inside the bawdy

    6. The Berri inside the metro body

    7. The body breaking free

BODY OF WORK

I. [Untitled]

Walk through [   ] where a mallard homes [ ]self in catkin nest. The girls
[ ] at work. They wash their feet [ ] a porcelain basin whenever their
lunch break comes, to rinse off [ ] mold that grows under their [   ] desks.
Grandmother gives me [ ] handful of desiccated water lilies. I am to gift
them [ ] the long-stemmed girls as a [   ]of peace and good [   ]. I am
grateful. The cool water [   ] my ankles; the fountain does not run.
Laughter of ducks. [   ] is paces [   ] , barefoot in pond. She announces
[ ] afternoon's radio programme will feature my [   ]. It [   ] be
broadcasted through [ ] park's loudspeakers—the ones [   ] reserved
for [   ]   [   ] hits. Her proud voice at [ ] nape [   ], *Listen.*

II. Torso

Allergic reaction
left me pink,
an English rose
farine-five
electric blossoming.

Cold cream won't galvanize
the swelling petals
of cheek,
but change is growth, always.

Tell me I'm wrong.
Tell me
sensitive skin
is an over-the-counter odyssey,
a sap-rich trek to where we're taught

to replace "reaction" with response.
That I need sex that calms
like an antihistamine.
The side effect of untreated thorns:
I only love
when I'm anaphylactic.

III. Osculation

Contacted two curves
at the traffic light
of their common tangent
[euphemism]

I [never kiss and] tell

IV. Morbid Intrusion

[*The gavel bangs. The ensuing silence is a cloister.*]

> Hear, hear, little lady—
> you ought to have stayed in the domestic sphere.

No one puts my baby in a corner.

> We find the defendant guilty of narrative scythes,
> agoraphobia en masse,
> and condemning each skylight as though
> it were a glass ceiling.
> We'll take a brief recess before unspooling further.

[*He pulls her aside.*]

The greatest thing you'll ever learn is just to love
and be loved in return.
Confess (to crossing the line and we'll swap litigation
for delineation, meaning
we'll draw your chalk outline on the ground and you'll
publicly acknowledge
gaslighting as preferable to the electric stove. I'll round you out
and bring home the bacon,
and you'll put your degrees toward something with use—
homeschooling the kids.)

I'm asking you to settle in court.
I'm asking you to marry me, you little fool.

V. Posture

Incipit [incision]
Chronicle [try-fail cycles]
Lines [little deaths]
Forming an utterance [otherworld]
Victim [sacrifice]
Bystander [self-defence]
Bitch [poison]
Denotation [I broke]
Connotation [my mirror's turn to shatter]
Vice [vise]
Greeting [guts]
Forgiveness [understand]
Arrogance [collective noun for all I refuse]
Redaction [sick]

VI. Paint Stripper

When my number begins, the crowd goes wild.
Burnt flakes of burnt umber drift down like confetti,
at the start of a wedding. Pull a string
and watch me come apart.
Book un-binded, un-remembered,
un-reminded. A subcutaneous striptease.
All matchmakers are arsonists
at heart. Wood pulped for reading or chipped
for striking newsprint until it catches. Caustic

ash. It's hot enough now,
I've removed my topcoat. Your dustjacket
is draped across a bar stool.
With this pigment gone, what remains is ekphrasis:
octopus tree, a sketch titled *World Peace*,
a single lung of lighter fluid. No covers, no canvas.
Tonight this money burns a hole
where your pocket ought to be.

Barefaced, the inner leaf. Pristine and artless,
a paper doll cut from the table of contents,
my tongue a bookmark so when they come again
I'll remember their place.

VII. Dehiscent

R is for role play:

you be the Republican
to my bleeding heart.

Start by releasing your seeds
in my home and native land.

There's nothing sexier than a bully
rupturing my borders,
filibustering my every—

Gerrymander me.

        [Ungracious me
                sharing a fantasy that enables
                      my control
                through the split-wound
                  choosing of a side.
        My weakness—

                  I cannot but disperse
                    my contents.]

VIII. Voyeur's Curse

[Cast (off) iron(s) pan handled.]
Brindled [memory of a hard drive] to succeed.

[To those (who (choose to)) watch us while we sleep—]

You'll see as you do.

[My gift to you is that] you will [never] know(.)

My own worst, in shackling this to the page.

IX. Forgery, Exhibitionist

Fooling me once is an incident

                [Shame on you]

                          Fooling me twice

is a coincidence

                          [Shame on me]

Fooling me three times

              is connect-the-dots

                          For a circle

  of Hell

[Omne trium perfectum]

X. Vise

[Hold me] wrong

XI. Sick

"I'm picking at my stitches.
You might say I'm well-red (sic)."

XII. Embrace

Stilted mettle, stemmed
intaglio asunder in your hand
the cut-vase glass
once squared in by the edge
of your copperplate
now aligns in crimson

a ledge
a brick dawn
a way back

DEBULKING

Cannot but ease suffering. Abate nausea with a wafer-thin splint.
Like bodybuilders' skin of glacé fruit, all sinew and sunbath.

Caricatures beachside of caloric consumption—arugula, arrowroot,
avocados galore. Lipo 'cause I'm on a budget and cheat days
risky as pain when you're in it to win it. To fail to die is to be

disqualified. I'm a tapered icon, uncorking micellar water
in celebration, creatine worth the stomach aches more so
than colostomy, catheter, tape worm.

Medals at the illness centre. A game of fresh sheets.
Mass effect. Palliative touch of duvet on flesh.

INANIMATE WHOSE

Use every trick in the book. Buy a dictionary then rip out all its pages.
Attend a séance for burglars. Be afraid of ghosts. Get possessed
by your own furniture. Grab the listless breeze, neglect the photograph
of a mundane breakfast. Throw out what doesn't bring you joy.

Follow your…Are you following? Drop the act—the secularized landscape,
the disembodied genitive, the modern folk-belief of resectable spirit.
Meditate in not on it. Treat your unhinging with CBD oil. Walk a mile
in something else's shoes. I'm not saying hold hands, but forget the lamp,

ottoman, tinder fungus, blade of grass and you miss the tip-off.
CBT for the soul. Chicken soup for your grammar-check. Subsistence.
The only respectable response is holistic: mind, body, ambience.

THE MYTHIC IS A MEANS TO AN END

The sphinx ought to have stopped Oedipus
                    in his tracks, cleaning up a bloodline
messier than a broken bottle

                    of extra-virgin olive oil on Aisle 4.
                              Happiness is not an ideal of reason,
                    but of imagination, skyscrapers leer,

star-spangled tarot cards in hand,
                              cuspids reflecting the sun's sullen gaze
in squares of rose gold, ice blue, gunmetal.

                    Scry a world that waits;
                              children on crowded corners
                    the prophets of tomorrow's cat's

cradle. Enigma isn't a tall, dark and handsome;
                              it's an ouroboros, a clam-bellied snake
choking itself blind in the throes

                    of asphyxiated fable.
                              We love the ones that drive us wild,
                    inevitable as a myopic red riding hood

raising juvenile knuckles
                    to rap on a door flayed open
                              by the claws of a wolf.

UNOPENED LOVE LETTERS

Emblem, I unfurl into new fractals.
An arm, a leg, no longer vapid air
or porous rock, but hunks of glittering ore
unrolling pink as the inner eyelid,

noticed for the very first time. See the
curtain for its ability to shade, the sun's
attentiveness an issue no longer. My legs
open to blossom, each petal a lace wing

to fly a kite on. See how open, how blue
it is from above the world's cotton
ceiling. I loosen the silk of my soul-shift;
it's too everything up here to think of snow

or answers. Too oxygen-rich to be
grateful for having genuflected, touching
flesh to concrete because I wanted to be
pure as light through a church window. Pane-

-free. What is transcendence from a height
birds envy? Splaying my corners to the winds
I finger the sky until it comes. Hard. *Rain,
rain, go away*…This is the real gift.

NOTES

"The Diagrammatic and Artistic Representation of Cannibalism and Psychopomps" is a play on the title of John Venn's essay, "On the Diagrammatic and Mechanical Representation of Propositions and Reasonings."

"Four Humouresques" contains allusions to the following pieces of popular music: Carly Simon's "You're So Vain;" The Undisputed Truth's "Papa Was a Rollin' Stone;" Cher's "Bang Bang (My Baby Shot Me Down);" and Guns N' Roses' "Cold November Rain."

"The Baldwin Affect" is a play on "The Baldwin Effect" from evolutionary biology.

The line "A printshop girl with Academy Award armpits" in "On Autopsies" and the reference in "Flora" to "my vegetable laughter" riff off Elizabeth Smart's *By Grand Central Station I Sat Down and Wept*. I owe "Religion exists only if it is performed" which appears in "On Autopsies" to Bill Gladhill, who taught CLAS 380, the notes from which contain this line.

The quote at the beginning of "On Scar Tissue" is from Andrew Lang's version of "King Lindorm" in *The Pink Fairy Book*. The line "unbinds in seven sheaths" is a reference to Vesalius' *De Humani Corporis Fabrica Libri Septem*.

A line in "What Follows Next" alludes to The Beatles' "Blackbird." "Ruin, Legacy" references A. J. M. Smith's "The Lonely Land" and Canadian literary critic Northrop Frye.

"Lichtenberg Figure" pulls lines from the traditional folksongs "Lavender's Blue" and "Scarborough Fair." The Minecraft Wiki entry for "Lightning" was another source.

"Placeholder, I Call Thee By Thy Name" references Antti Aarne and Stith Thompson's classification system for folktales, as well as the nursery rhymes "This Is the House That Jack Built" and "Who Killed Cock Robin," and the fairy tale, "The Juniper Tree."

"Northern Hemisphere" and "Southern Hemisphere" were inspired by an NPR interview with Iain McGilchrist. Last line in "Southern Hemisphere" is from Coriolanus, Act 3, Scene 2.

"Temporal Lobe" riffs on the line "and later cried myself to sleep" from Ken Babstock's "Compatibilist."

The found poem, "On Antediluvians" is composed of modified phrases from CATIE (Canada's source for HIV and Hepatitis C information) and the Book of Job, Chapter 2 (*KJV*).

"Xenia's Oath" is a bastardized copy of an English translation of The Hippocratic Oath.

"Reproduced" references Gertrude Stein's "Rose is a rose is a rose is a rose."

"Morbid Intrusion" contains quotes from *Dirty Dancing*, *Moulin Rouge* (from a Nat King Cole song written by eden ahbez), and Daphne du Maurier's *Rebecca*.

"The Mythic is a Means to An End" quotes Immanuel Kant: "Happiness is not an ideal of reason, but of imagination."

"Unopened Love Letter" is a response to Sylvia Plath's "Love Letter."

"On Insides" appeared in *The Dalhousie Review*.

"Occipital Lobe" is forthcoming in *Hamilton Arts & Letters*.

"On Autopsies" appeared in The Selkie's *Very Much Alive: Stories of Resilience*.

"On Vertices" appeared in *yolk literary*.

"Placeholder, I Call Thee By Thy Name" appeared in *Lantern Magazine*.

"Half-Life, Love, Hyphen" was written for *CIME*'s 2020 fundraiser.

Poems selected from this manuscript were published by Cactus Press as a chapbook, *Xenia* (2021).

ACKNOWLEDGEMENTS

My gratitude to:

Devon Gallant at Cactus Press, for making this dream a reality; James Dunnigan, for believing in my work when I yet didn't; David Drummond, for the lovely cover; the Caesura Collective for friendship and warmth and never holding back: Jerome Ramcharitar, Derek Godin, Jacalyn Den Haan, Mariana Jiménez, John William Wither, christian favreau, Frances Pope, Andrew Stewart, Peter Jermyn, Aris Keshav, Margot Cozens, Carolyne Van Der Meer, and Laura Chan.

Friends who read the manuscript: Samara Garfinkle for constructive and honest criticism; Matthew Rettino for challenging my (limited) knowledge of firearms; and Avleen K. Mokha (Mirabel), for the best handwritten notes. This book is better because of the keen eyes of Norman Cristofoli and Brandon Pitts. Thank you, Bryan Sentes and George Slobodzian for egging me on.

The Art Accountability pandemic group: Isaac Maynes, Bashu Naimi-Roy, Mykl Ó Nualláin, Gabriel Frank, and Kieran Camellia-Sinensis. I was ill throughout 2020. Those bi-weekly meetings kept my spirit alive.
Helge Dascher, for encouraging emails and a kitchen talk on the importance of valuing your work, Christopher Pearson for science, and Bill Gladhill, whose McGill course on Ancient Greek worldview spurred me to write the earliest draft of this book.

Chris Lyons at the McGill Rare Books Library, who spoke with such excitement about Vesalius, Galen, and the history of anatomical manuscripts that it was impossible not to be inspired. This book wouldn't exist without those afternoons at ROAAr events.

Zach Buck, for a dog walk in the rain and a recitation.

Hack Laureates—Sijia Li, Alex Keys, and Taylor Gray-Moore.
Patrick "Octopodes" O'Reilly, Lisa Banks, Annie, and Sam—my favourite feline muse.

My international writer pals: Oscar Hjelmstedt, Josh Penna, Kurt Slauson, Ahsan Yousaf, Deven Rieck.

Tomas Griffin, Apollonia Griffin, Cole Griffin, Christopher Junn, Boris "Lacuna" But, Emily Crompton, Chloë Zaffran, Andrew Gordon Middleton, Hamish Savage, and Cassian Bopp, who let me sic early drafts on them.

Friends who lent ears, shoulders, hearts: Meike Peters-Lauzon, Yalda Jahandideh, Jacqueline Frehner, and Bree Rockbrand.

Those who nurtured me with their art, kindness, and/or food: Amanda Lenko, Dolly Lanuza, Christine McLean, Mathieu Lamarre, Ian Rodgers, Curtis McRae, Buddha Biswas, Oliver Golt Brunet, Ennie Gloom, Atsushi Ikeda, Cairn Tse-Lalonde, Justin "Gio-Gio" Toppetta-Marino, Liam Thomas, Adrian Bambace, and Malavy Moeun.

Jaëlle Dutremble-Rivet. Dear friend, thank you.

My family: my mother, JC, who encouraged my creativity and "leadership qualities;" my father, Oisín, who read to child-me until he fell asleep most nights; my brother, Merlin; and sister Finn. My Nonna, Beatrice Pearson and my granny, Ginni Little—for tales of faerie and family. Nancy Marrelli and Simon Dardick, for support navigating the Canadian literary scene and cups of tea with ginger syrup.

I don't know what I did in a past life to deserve such wonderful friends and family. My gratitude is bone-deep.

ABOUT THE AUTHOR

Willow Loveday Little is a British-Canadian writer. She lives in Montreal where she works as a freelance editor and English teacher. *(Vice) Viscera* is her first full-length poetry collection. Visit her @willowloveday.

CACTUS PRESS